Our Street I

MARGARET MARIS

Picture Knight

British Library Cataloguing in Publication Data
Maris, Margaret
Our street party.
I. Title
823'.914[J]   PZ7
ISBN 0–340–42615–5

Copyright © Margaret Maris 1987

First published 1987 by Julia MacRae Books
This edition first published 1988 by Picture Knight

Published by Hodder and Stoughton Paperbacks,
a division of Hodder and Stoughton Ltd,
Mill Road, Dunton Green, Sevenoaks, Kent TN13 2YE
Editorial office: 47 Bedford Square, London WC1E 3DP

Printed in Great Britain by Cambus Litho, East Kilbride

All rights reserved

For Julia

Where are you going, Little Mouse?
"We're going to the street party."

Who else will be there?

"Rocket and Witch . . .

... and here comes Clown."

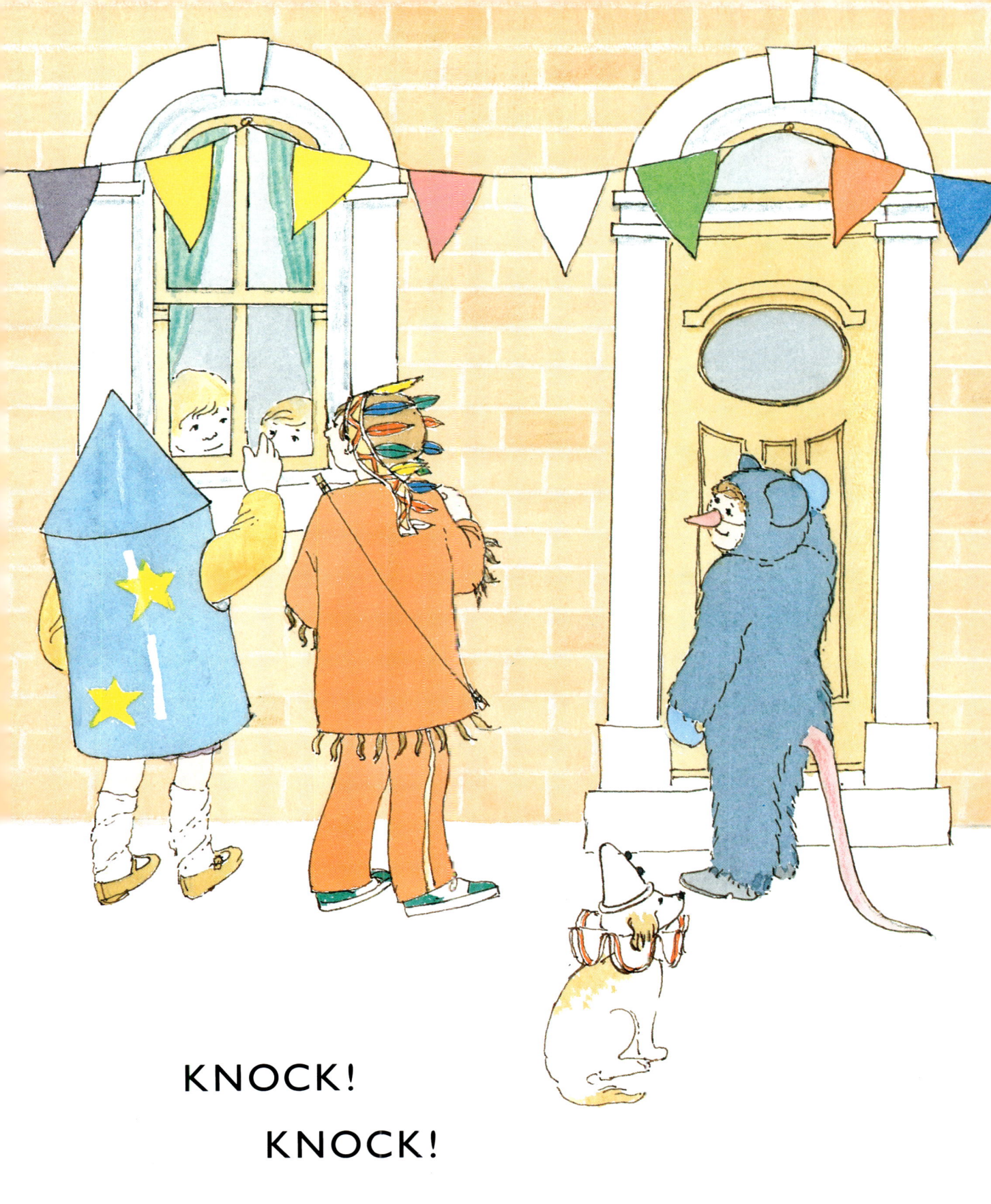

"Tom and Tessa have measles.
They can't come to the street party."

"Do you all like balloons?"

"Oh, oh, my balloon . . .
it's blown away!"

"Don't cry, Little Mouse, here's another one for you."

"What are you doing, Little Mouse?"

"I'm bouncing much higher than anyone."

"Come on, let's have tea!"

"We'll all follow Little Mouse."

"There's plenty to eat for everyone."

"But where is Little Mouse?"

"He's not behind the tree."

"He's not inside the bin."

"Has he gone home?"

"No, *here* he is!"

It's time to go home.
"Thank you for a lovely party."

"Here's tea for Tom and Tessa.
We hope they soon feel better."

"Goodnight, Little Mouse. It's been a great party."

"We gave them to all our friends.
Even Little Mouse!"

"Hello, Tom and Tessa. Where are your spots?"